W9-BCO-472

Butterfield School
Learning Center
1441 W. Lake Street
Libertyville, IL 60048

DEMCO

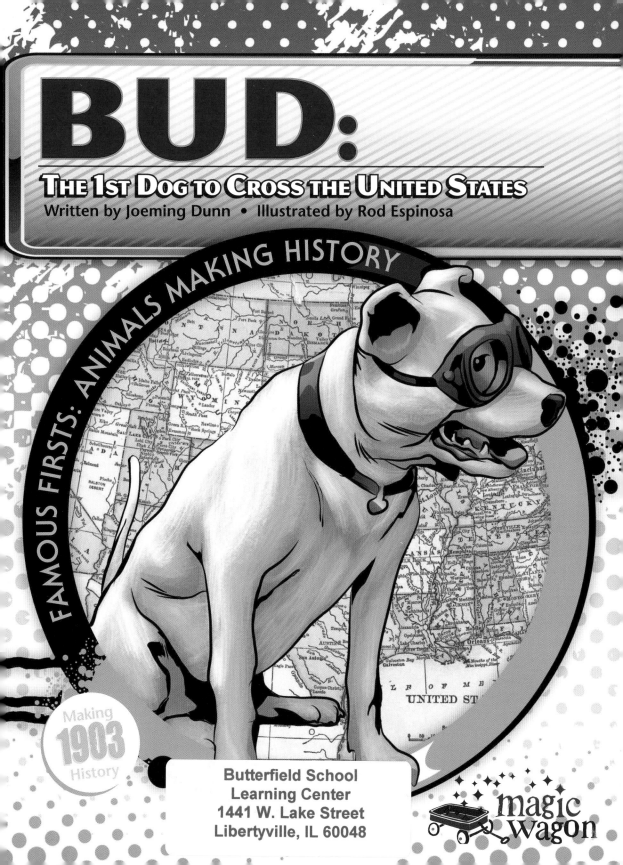

BUD:

THE 1ST DOG TO CROSS THE UNITED STATES

Written by Joeming Dunn • Illustrated by Rod Espinosa

FAMOUS FIRSTS: ANIMALS MAKING HISTORY

Making 1903 History

Butterfield School
Learning Center
1441 W. Lake Street
Libertyville, IL 60048

magic wagon

visit us at www.abdopublishing.com

Published by Magic Wagon, a division of the ABDO Publishing Group, 8000 West 78th Street, Edina, Minnesota 55439. Copyright © 2012 by Abdo Consulting Group, Inc. International copyrights reserved in all countries. All rights reserved. No part of this book may be reproduced in any form without written permission from the publisher.

Graphic Planet™ is a trademark and logo of Magic Wagon.

Printed in the United States of America, North Mankato, Minnesota.
052011
092011
This book contains at least 10% recycled materials.

Written by Joeming Dunn
Illustrated and colored by Rod Espinosa
Lettered by Rod Espinosa
Edited by Stephanie Hedlund and Rochelle Baltzer
Interior layout and design by Antarctic Press
Cover art by Brian Denham
Cover design by Neil Klinepier

Library of Congress Cataloging-in-Publication Data

Dunn, Joeming W.
  Bud : the 1st dog to cross the United States / written by Joeming Dunn ; illustrated by Rod Espinosa.
     p. cm. -- (Famous firsts. Animals making history)
  Includes index.
  ISBN 978-1-61641-638-6
  1. American bulldog--United States--Anecdotes. I. Espinosa, Rod, ill. II. Title.
  SF429.B85D96 2012
  636.72--dc22
                              2011011362

TABLE OF CONTENTS

THE HORSELESS CARRIAGE

Before there were cars, most people traveled by walking, riding horses, or sailing boats.

Each of these travel options had its limits.

After the steam engine was made, things began to change. Soon, people and cargo could be moved long distances with locomotive engines.

Steam locomotives solved many problems. Yet there were places where railroad tracks simply could not be built.

People began dreaming of self-propelled personal transportation.

Many people worked to build the automobile. But German scientist Karl Benz created the first gasoline-powered internal combustion engine.

IN JANUARY 1886, BENZ WAS GRANTED A PATENT FOR HIS CREATION. HE STARTED PRODUCTION IN 1888.

Soon, more people were making automobiles. In the United States, Duryea Motor Company, Olds Motor Vehicle Company, and the Ford Motor Company began producing cars.

Alexander Winton was another early automobile manufacturer.

Winton was a Scottish immigrant who lived in Cleveland, Ohio. He got his start as a bicycle builder.

Winton released his first car in 1897.

Many people doubted Winton's automobile, so he decided to prove them wrong.

He drove his car 800 miles (1,287 km) from Cleveland to New York City, New York!

The Winton Motor Carriage Company's automobiles became very popular. Wealthy people, such as Reginald and Alfred Vanderbilt, became customers.

More and more automobiles became available. Yet roads and bridges cars needed were slow to catch up.

THE BET

In the 1800s, people disagreed about the usefulness of automobiles. Some claimed they were just noisy problems.

Others believed they were a toy that would soon be forgotten.

Dr. Horatio Nelson Jackson was a supporter of the automobile.

AND MY SOON-TO-BE OWNER!

Dr. Jackson and his wife, Bertha, were very wealthy. They loved to travel.

9

In spring 1903, the Jacksons were vacationing in San Francisco, California.

During the vacation, the Jacksons both took driving lessons.

One evening, Dr. Jackson went to San Francisco's University Club. While there, he and several others began talking about automobiles.

THESE AUTOMOBILES ARE JUST PLAYTHINGS. THEY'RE NOT USEFUL AT ALL.

I DISAGREE! I THINK THEIR USEFULNESS IS JUST BEGINNING TO TAKE SHAPE.

PSHAW! YOU ARE FOOLISH TO BELIEVE SUCH THINGS.

Dr. Jackson knew very little about cars. So, he asked a young chauffeur named Sewall Crocker to be his mechanic and backup driver.

Crocker convinced Jackson that he should buy a Winton car. So, he bought a slightly used one.

I SHALL NAME THIS CAR VERMONT, AFTER MY HOME STATE.

Soon, Jackson and Crocker began preparing for their trip. The first thing thing they did was get a spare tire. They found only one in all of San Francisco!

Jackson and Crocker gathered everything they would need for their trip. That included sleeping bags, spare parts, tools, and gasoline cans.

They knew the trip would be long and challenging. The Vermont's top speed was about 30 miles per hour (48 km/h).

At the time, there were very few paved roads.

And there were no gas or service stations along the way.

Since there were no road maps, the pair carefully studied maps of the terrain. They were looking for a good place to cross the country.

Alexander Winton had already tried to make a cross-country trip in one of his cars…

…only to be stopped by the deserts of Nevada…

…and the towering Rocky Mountains.

Jackson and Crocker decided to follow the Oregon Trail, which was a more northern route.

THE JOURNEY BEGINS

On May 23, 1903, Jackson and Crocker started their trip.

The car went by ferry from San Francisco to Oakland, California.

Then, the pair drove east toward California's capital, Sacramento.

POP!
BLAM!

Just 15 miles (24 km) into their journey, Jackson and Crocker had to use their only spare tire.

A BLOWN TIRE WAS JUST THE FIRST OF MANY PROBLEMS!

The sidelights were too dim for night driving and needed to be replaced.

And without any more spare tires, they had to use inner tubes for any flats.

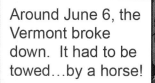
Around June 6, the Vermont broke down. It had to be towed…by a horse!

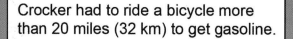
While fixing the car, Crocker discovered a fuel leak.

Crocker had to ride a bicycle more than 20 miles (32 km) to get gasoline.

Then around June 9, the car ran out of oil.

To get some oil, Jackson headed back to the last town they had visited. It was many miles away.

Jackson discovered there was a town much closer in the other direction.

OLD
←TOWN
2 MILES

IF ONLY HE'D HAD A ROAD MAP!

The pair made it to Ontario, Oregon. There, they were able to get more supplies.

After Oregon, their journey brought them to Caldwell, Idaho.

CALDWELL IDAHO

That's when my adventure began!

The Winton had no windshield to block the dust from the dirt roads. So when my journey started, the dust really bothered my eyes. Luckily, my owner knew just what to do!

Jackson put goggles on me as if I were human! Soon, I got so used to the goggles that I wouldn't start a day of driving without them.

One time, a woman gave them wrong directions...

...just so her friends and family could see a car!

Now and then, they would have to lift the car across deep streams...

...or pay to cross someone's property.

21

Everyone marveled at my traveling skills.

At stops, my master would leave me in the front seat as a watchdog.

GRRRRRR!

I even learned to be ready for a turn and lean the right direction.

Things went very well, except I got sick once from drinking bad water.

Bad luck hit us in Wyoming. A heavy rainstorm forced us to change direction.

We had to avoid areas that had flooded.

One time, we ran out of money. So, my master had to sell his watch for $10.

Luckily, my master's wife could send money whenever we got around a telegraph office.

23

The telegraph was very important to us. It allowed us to get money. It also allowed us to contact the Winton Motor Carriage Company for parts!

It provided news of our exciting journey, too. As the news traveled, we became famous! People lined up along the road to catch sight of us as we passed.

On July 12, we drove more than 250 miles (402 km) through Nebraska with a broken axle. Fortunately, a blacksmith fixed it in Omaha.

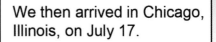

We then arrived in Chicago, Illinois, on July 17.

I decided to take a personal tour of Chicago. My master had to chase me down before we could leave town!

We had quite a following by then. We led a whole line of cars out of Chicago and almost to Indiana!

We kept driving, even in heavy rains. Luckily, the roads were a bit better in this area of the country.

On July 21, we arrived in Buffalo, New York.

We could see the end of our adventure. So, we decided to drive well into the night.

This may not have been our best decision. We had our first accident of the entire trip! Luckily no one, not even the Vermont, was hurt badly.

Finishing our trip was not the only reason we wanted to continue. We discovered that the Packard Motor Car Company had sponsored Tom Fetch and Marius Krarup to make the same trip. They had left San Francisco on June 20.

It wasn't an official race, but we still wanted to finish first!

At 4:30 a.m. on July 26, we pulled into New York City. We became the first group to cross the United States in an automobile! It took us 63 days, 12 hours, and 30 minutes. Fetch and Krarup made the trip in less time, but we arrived first!

I met my master's wife, Bertha, for the first time. She had taken the train back from San Francisco and met us in New York.

The entire trip cost $8,000, which is almost $200,000 in today's money. It's a good thing my master was wealthy.

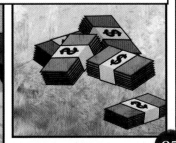

Dr. Horatio Nelson Jackson, Sewell Crocker, and I, Bud the Bulldog, will always be remembered in American history as the first to make a transcontinental automobile trip. We all helped prove that the car was not just a passing fad but a useful tool.

The Vermont and my goggles can now be found in the Smithsonian Institution in Washington DC.

BUD FACTS

Name: Bud
Age at the time of the journey: 1 to 2 years old
Weight: Unknown
Breed: American bulldog

Making **1903** History

Starting point: Bud joined the journey near Caldwell, Idaho, on June 12, 1903.
Ending point: Bud and the men reached New York City, New York, on July 26, 1903.

Result: Bud became the first dog to make a transcontinental automobile trip. This trip helped prove that the car was not just a passing fad but a useful tool.

WEB SITES

To learn more about Bud, visit ABDO Group online at **www.abdopublishing.com**. Web sites about Bud are featured on our Book Links page. These links are routinely monitored and updated to provide the most current information available.

GLOSSARY

axle – a shaft or a bar on which wheels revolve.

cargo – something that is carried from one place to another, especially by boat, train, or airplane.

chauffeur – a person who drives an automobile to transport others.

ferry – a boat used to carry people, goods, and automobiles across a body of water.

immigrant – a person who enters another country to live.

internal combustion engine – a heat engine that has the burning take place inside an engine instead of a furnace.

locomotive – an engine that moves under its own power and is used to pull trains.

mascot – something to bring good luck.

mechanic – a person who repairs machines.

patent – the exclusive right granted to a person to make or sell an invention. This right lasts for a certain period of time.

paved – covered with a material, such as tar, to make a level surface for travel.

propel – to drive forward or onward by some force.

regret – the feeling of being sorry for something you did or did not do.

route – a road or course that has been traveled or will be traveled.

sponsor – to support someone, often financially.

telegraph – a device that uses electricity to send coded messages over wires.

transcontinental – crossing a continent.

transportation – the act of moving things from one place to another.

INDEX